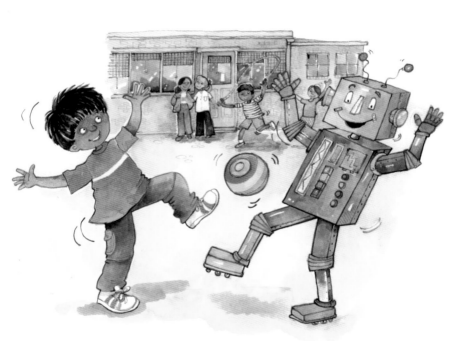

⌀ Dominie Press, Inc.

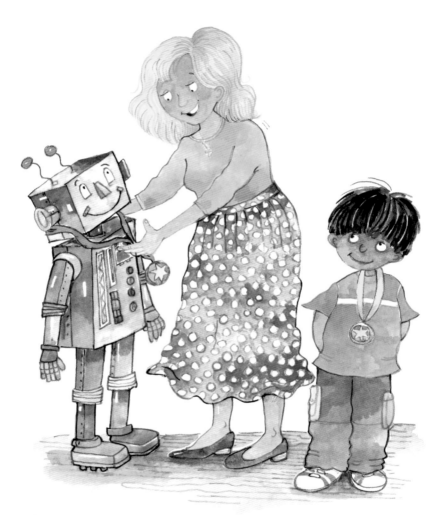

My robot is good at school.

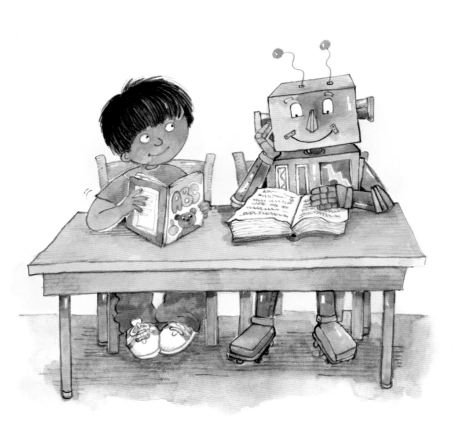

He is good at reading.

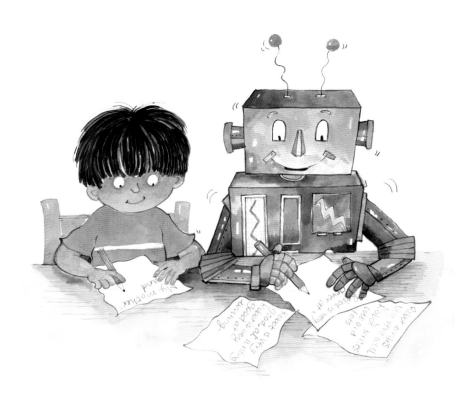

He is good at writing.

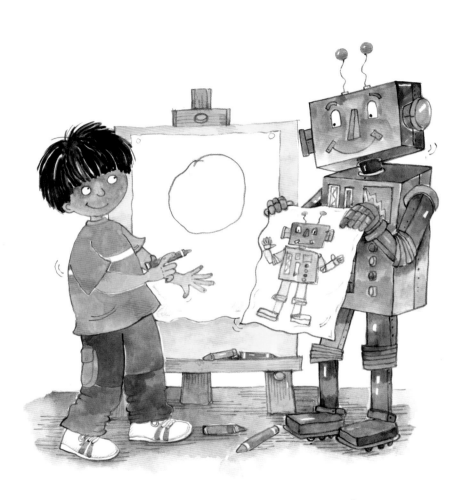

He is good at drawing.

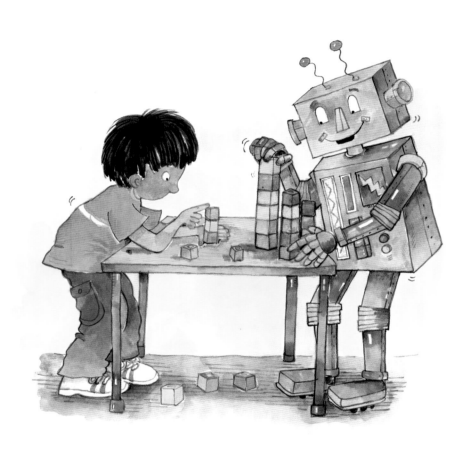

He is good at counting.

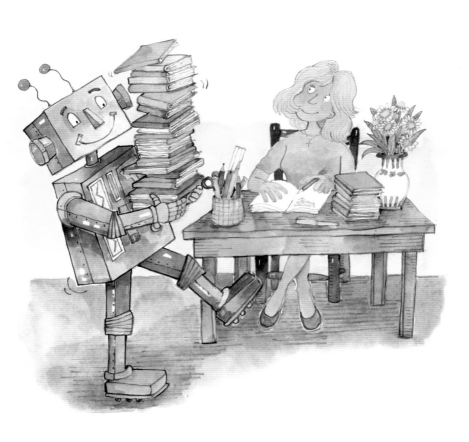

He is good at helping.

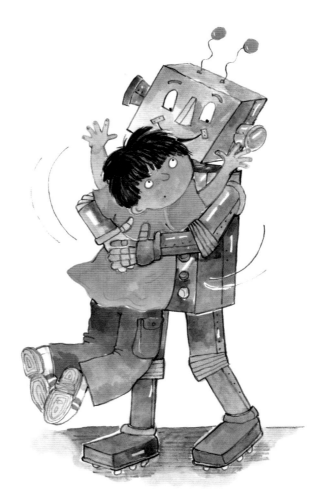

But he is not good
at hugging.